Snow
Leopards

Victoria Blakemore

For Aunt Alison, with love

© 2018 Victoria Blakemore

Copyright info/picture credits

Table of Contents

What Are Snow Leopards?

Snow leopards are large mammals. Although they are called leopards, they are actually more closely related to tigers.

Researchers believe that there are two kinds of snow leopards. They differ in where they live.

They are usually gray, cream,

and white in color. Like leopards,

they have black **rosettes**.

Size

Snow leopards are usually between three and four feet long. Their tail adds another three feet to their length.

When fully grown, snow leopards usually weigh between seventy-five and one hundred twenty pounds.

Male snow leopards are

usually larger than female

snow leopards.

Physical Characteristics

Snow leopards often have light green or gray eyes. This is different from other large cats, that usually have yellow eyes.

They have a long, thick tail. Their tail helps them to balance as they move among the rocks and over the snow.

Snow leopards have a thick coat of fur in the winter. In the summer, their coat is thinner so they don't **overheat**.

Habitat

Snow leopards are found at high **altitudes** in the mountains. They are usually seen on cliffs and among the rocks.

It is very cold where they live and it often snows there. However, snow leopards are usually found lower than where there is always snow.

Range

Snow leopards are only found in the mountains of Central Asia.

They are found in countries like Russia, China, Kazakhstan, India, and Afghanistan.

Diet

Snow leopards are **carnivores**. This means that they eat only meat.

Their diet is made up of wild sheep and goats. They have also been known to eat deer, birds, and other small mammals.

The color of their fur helps snow leopards to sneak up on their prey.

Snow leopards usually hunt alone, but are sometimes seen hunting in pairs. When alone, they sneak up on their prey.

When they hunt in pairs, one snow leopard hides and waits. The other snow leopard tries to get the prey to come close enough for the hidden leopard to catch it.

When snow leopards catch

large prey, they stay close by so

they can eat it for several days.

Communication

Snow leopards use sound and scent to communicate. They make sounds like growls, chuffs, hisses, mewls, and purrs.

They mark their territory with their scent by rubbing on trees. They also use their claws to scratch tree bark and rocks.

The shape of a snow leopards

throat prevents them from

being able to roar.

Movement

Snow leopards have very large, wide paws. This helps them to walk easily on the snow. Their paws have fur on the bottom so they stay warm.

They are fast and can run at speeds of up to fifty-five miles per hour. This is only for short distances.

They are able to pounce far and

fast. They can leap up to thirty

feet in one jump.

Snow Leopard Cubs

Snow leopards usually have a

litter of two or three babies.

The babies are called cubs.

They are born with their eyes

closed.

When cubs are young, their fur

is darker than their parents fur.

It lightens up as they get older.

Cubs live with their mother for nearly two years. She teaches them how to hunt for food.

Snow Leopard Life

Snow leopards tend to be **solitary**. They spend most of their time alone. When they are seen together, it is usually a mother and her cubs.

They have been known to follow the **migrations** of their prey, moving as the weather gets warmer.

Snow leopards are **crepuscular**.

They are most active at dawn

and at dusk.

The Ghost of the Mountain

Snow leopards are sometimes called ghosts of the mountains. This is because they are hard to find and seem to disappear into the snow.

Their spots get lighter to help them blend in to the snow, making them hard to find in the winter.

Snow leopards are usually very shy and avoid humans. This is another reason why they are hard to find.

Population

Snow leopards are **vulnerable**.
There are not many left. They
could become **endangered** if
their population **declines**.

They are shy and stay away
from humans, so they are hard
to count. There are thought to
be fewer than 7,500 left in the
wild.

In the wild, snow leopards often

live between ten and thirteen

years. They can live longer in

captivity.

Snow Leopards in Danger

Snow leopards have been hunted by people for many years. They are usually hunted for their fur.

Sometimes, they are hunted for their bones. In some parts of Asia, their bones and teeth are used to make medicines.

They are also in danger due to

conflict with people who keep

livestock in their habitats.

Helping Snow Leopards

There are many people trying to help snow leopards. In many places it is **illegal** to hunt snow leopards. Some countries also have special rangers who watch for **poachers**.

Special protected areas have been set up to provide snow leopards with a safe habitat.

Some groups are working with **livestock** herders. They want to try to reduce the amount of **conflict** between people and snow leopards.

Researchers are studying snow leopards and tracking their population. They want to make sure that their populations do not **decline**.

Glossary

Altitudes: the height of a place or thing above sea level

Captivity: animals that are kept by humans, not in the wild

Carnivore: an animal that eats only meat

Conflict: fight or disagreement

Crepuscular: when an animal is most active at dawn and dusk

Declining: getting smaller

Endangered: at risk of becoming extinct

Illegal: against the law

Litter: a group of animals born at the same time

Livestock: animals such as cows or sheep that are kept by humans

Migrations: when animals move from place to place due to the weather or food

Overheat: to become too hot

Poacher: someone who hunts an animal illegally

Rosettes: spots that are circular and look like roses

Solitary: living alone

Vulnerable: when an animal may become endangered if the population declines

About the Author

Victoria Blakemore is a first grade

teacher in Southwest Florida with a

passion for reading.

You can visit her at

www.elementaryexplorers.com

Also in This Series

Gray Wolves · Sloths · Flamingos · Camels · Koalas · Honey Bees · Pandas

Pangolins · White-Tailed Deer · Orcas · Giraffes · Corn · Meerkats · Echidnas

Walruses · Raccoons · Bald Eagles · Apples · Arctic Foxes · Red Pandas · Cassowaries

Tigers · Ladybugs · Moose · Beluga Whales · Leopards · Elephants · Jellyfish

Binturongs · Lions · Dolphins · Reindeer · Hammerhead Sharks · Hippos · Pumpkins

Peafowl · Chameleons · Florida Panthers · Aye-Ayes · Black Bears · Cheetahs · Manatees

Gingerbread · Polar Bears · Hot Chocolate · Orangutans · Coyotes · Marshmallows · Strawberries

Victoria Blakemore

Also in This Series

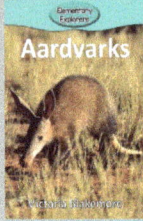

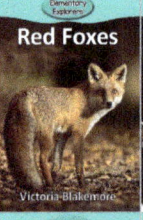

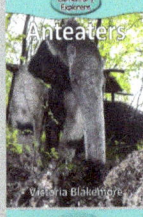

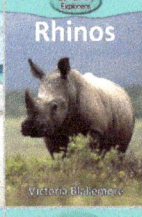

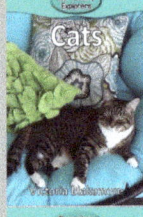

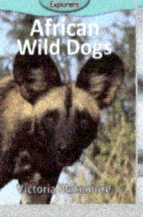

Aardvarks	**Mako Sharks**	**Alligators**	**Frogs**	**Hedgehogs**	**Brown Bears**	**Bongos**
Sea Turtles	**Quokkas**	**Muskrats**	**Zebras**	**Red Foxes**	**Ring-Tailed Lemurs**	**Platypuses**
Anteaters	**Kangaroos**	**Rhinos**	**Jaguars**	**Wombats**	**Capybaras**	**Gorillas**
Cats	**Skunks**	**Butterflies**	**Dingoes**	**Snow Leopards**	**African Wild Dogs**	**Penguins**
Whale Sharks	**Wolverines**	**Warthogs**	**Caracals**			

Victoria Blakemore

www.ingramcontent.com/pod-product-compliance
Lightning Source LLC
Chambersburg PA
CBHW051254020426

42333CB00025B/3199